This book belongs to

....

....

....

For Lili, my beautiful inspiration
For Tao and Maé. And for Sandrine, a thousand thank yous

Little Unicorn is
ANGRY

Aurélie Chien Chow Chine

Buster Books

This is **Little Unicorn**. Most of the time he is just like every other unicorn ... well, almost.

Sometimes **Little Unicorn** is happy.

Sometimes he is unhappy.

Sometimes he is sad.

Sometimes he is scared.

Sometimes he is angry.

These are feelings.

And, just like you, **Little Unicorn** has all kinds of feelings.

But **Little Unicorn** has one thing
that makes him magical:

his mane.

When he is having a good day, his mane
twinkles with all the colours of the rainbow.

But when things aren't going well, his mane
changes colour to match how he is feeling.

Happy
Jealous
Angry
Guilty

Shy
Scared
Sulky
Sad

How does **Little Unicorn** feel at the moment?

Terrible!

Oh dear. **Little Unicorn** feels terrible.
His heart hurts, like there's a big, black cloud in it.
He's going to tell us why.

What about you? How do you feel today?

Great

Good

Fine

Not good

Bad

Terrible

Why is **Little Unicorn** feeling so bad?

Most of the time, everything is great.
There isn't a cloud in the sky.

At home and at school,
Little Unicorn plays calmly.

But there are days when things just don't
work out like he wants them to.

And sometimes, that upsets **Little Unicorn**.

Like when he decides to go out and play
in the garden, but it suddenly starts to rain.
That makes **Little Unicorn** feel grumpy.

When he has to walk to school,
but he doesn't feel like walking,
it makes him grumpy.

And if Dad refuses to carry him,
Little Unicorn gets angry.

When Mummy calls **Little Unicorn** because it's bath time,
but he doesn't want to have a bath,
that makes him grumpy.

And when it's time to get out of the water,
but he still wants to play,
Little Unicorn gets angry.

When he wants to do something all on his own,
like a big unicorn would, but he finds things
don't turn out the way he wants,
that makes **Little Unicorn** grumpy.

Sometimes, he stamps his feet
and rolls around on the floor.

That's when he's feeling really **angry**.

Really, really angry!

It feels like there's a big, black cloud inside his head.
A cloud full of thunder and lightning.

What if he used a **breathing exercise**
to chase out that cloud, instead of waiting
for it to go away slowly on its own?

You can do it, too.
When you feel a cloud of anger is filling your head,
chase it away with this calming exercise.

A breathing exercise to chase away a cloud of anger

① **Little Unicorn** closes his eyes. He imagines the big, black cloud in his head. He breathes in through his nose, filling up his tummy with air. He stretches both arms down the length of his body and squeezes his hands into tight fists.

2 **Little Unicorn** holds his breath. He quickly shrugs his shoulders up and down a few times. It's like he is pumping all his anger up into the cloud.

3 Then **Little Unicorn** blows all the air out through his mouth and lets his shoulders and his hands go floppy. And, sure enough, the big cloud of anger is gone.

Little Unicorn does this breathing exercise **3 times**.

It takes at least 3 times to get all the
thunder and lightning to go away.

After that he can breathe calmly again.

Now that he has chased the cloud out of his head,
he can let the **sunshine** in.

Little Unicorn feels much better, and a lot calmer.
Now that he is feeling good, his mane
is all the colours of the rainbow again.

And next time things don't go the way he wants,
it's not a big deal. He can stay calm.

If you blow the cloud away and let
the sunshine in, like **Little Unicorn** did,
you might feel soothed and relaxed, too.
And your **smile** can come back!

Edited by Sylvie Michel and Hannah Daffern
Designed by Solène Lavand and cover designed by Angie Allison
Translation by Philippa Wingate

First published in Great Britain in 2019 by Buster Books,
an imprint of Michael O'Mara Books Limited, 9 Lion Yard, Tremadoc Road, London SW4 7NQ

W www.mombooks.com/buster   F Buster Books   T @BusterBooks

ISBN: 978-1-78055-642-0
2 4 6 8 10 9 7 5 3 1

This book was printed in August 2019 by Leo Paper Products Ltd, Heshan Astros Printing Limited,
Xuantan Temple Industrial Zone, Gulao Town, Heshan City, Guangdong Province, China.

Also available:

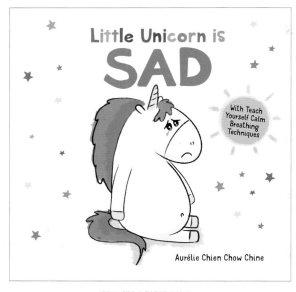

ISBN: 978-1-78055-643-7